A Universe of Love

Poetry by Deborah M. Hodgetts
Illustrations and Book Cover by Stewart Clough

A Universe of Love
Copyright © 2017 Deborah M. Hodgetts

The illustrations and book cover design
are by Stewart Clough.

Content page

Content Page

Content Page

Content Page

Content Page

Content Page

Content Page

Love is a million sparkling stars,
that guide me to you ...

This book is dedicated to the following twinkling stars:

This book is dedicated to my loving husband Maxwell, my beautiful daughter Phoebe, my wonderful Mum and Dad, my Sister and boys, and extended family: Mary, and my wonderful friends. Special thanks to Stewart Clough who visualised and created the beautiful Illustrations and the book cover – thank you!
Dianne, Eve, Naomi, Katie, Sam and Nikki. To all my friends around the World and the millions of stars who have lovingly guided, supported, watched, twinkled and followed me, encouraged me to the ends of the earth - I love you all with all my heart x

For with out you all there would be no Universe...
Each one of you sparkles bright with Love!

Thank you for A Universe of Love!

And to my Guardian Angels – I give my heartfelt thanks for watching me, believing in me and making this dream come true – I love you!

Forward

'A Universe of Love', takes you on a journey to the soul.

This is my journey, through poetry which I have been lovingly crafting and sharing on my blog 'The Beautiful Music of Words' for the last six years.

It is now time to share these poems with the world and so this book 'A Universe of Love' has been born.

Let the words, open you eyes and seep into every pore of your being.
Be transported into the heart of love and all of its complexities.

My hope is that these words will find you well, and take the dreariness away from your heavy eyes.

Eyes that sometimes do see the beauty of all that is love.
But in the humdrum of the day, get washed away and left on shelves to gather dust and decay.

The Universe is full of love, we as human's just need to open our eyes, hearts, minds and step in to the true wonder of life.

We are all but stardust, twinkling with love in a big bold Universe of Love!

Deborah x

I love you!

You are beautiful
The scent of a summers' day
The warmth of the sun
Lay by my side,
in the dewy grass
and let us drift away.

Let me hold your hand
Let me guide your footsteps,
 with gentle love.

For you are my beautiful
My one true love.

4

(This poem was inspired by my beautiful daughter, on being published at the age of 7)

Shine.

Deeply buried, kept from view.
Your shielded heart,
lies patiently beating in the dark.
Waiting for its moment to come.
And like a spark from a bright flickering flame;
you are illuminated.
You speak and rainbows of light burst forth.
For your words, bring you to life.
And now you shine!
Never, to be silent again.
Just shine, with true brilliance.
Child, of our time.
SHINE!

Sweet Child of mine.

Ten tiny fingers and ten tiny toes.
As she grips my finger.
Oh! What a beauteous rose.
Delicate, and perfect: a fragment of my heart.
A portion of my soul.

This diamond: flawless and whole.
My precious jewel, and my treasure to behold.
Limbs so small but formed sublime.
A blessing from heaven: this sweet child of
mine.

Lost Youth

Tiny packages, discarded
Litter dusty pavements.
Tears, wash dirt from tired eyes
Small fragile hands
Raised in hope for a few grains
to sate their hunger.
Our lost youth, left to decay
Long gone, they're happy yesterday
In shade they hide, under remnants
they find scattered around.
Sheltering from monsoon rains
For our greed, their lives they have paid
Their stolen dreams: our whitewashed memories.
Strewn careless, in the love they give.
Long lost: sweet child of India.

Mother: Pride

I planted you in my heart.
Long days of gentle nurture.
Lovingly sowing love,
into every molecule of your being.
Speaking to you as you grow within.
Dreaming about your future and all you can be.
Feeling your strength,
as you change my form.
Deep emotions growing
As soon our journey is to begin
And at last you are here.
And I your mother am very proud.
To shout how I love you very loud!

The Fragile Beauty of love

I hold you within the palm of my hand,
You rest within the creases of my palm
Small, perfect and wondrous in you're
magnificence to me.
If I were to drop you,
and you fell to the ground.
You would become what you need to be.
Find your wings and be free.

I hold you in my heart,
But know I cannot keep you.
Your love so fragile and so pure,
hangs like a silken thread.
So I will let you fall down,
down to the ground.
But as you fall,
I pray that the divine winds will carry you.
I pray that as you drift down,
that your landing will be sweetness and light.
For you are radiant,
and need to be free.

Come Home

We do not see eye to eye.
Like ships passing bye.
I wish you away, until
one day this love
has gone.
But deep in my heart,
a missing part,
wishes
simply wishes.
That you would come home,
back to this aching heart.
Simply signed with love.

The Robot Wife

I built you for a purpose
To serve me through my life
But then quite absurdly;
I asked you to be my wife.

Oh! Robot number 71 X 5 and 10

Why is it that I love you so?
Hard wired and made of tin,
Head from a dustbin,
And legs made of aluminium,
Washed up by the drag.
My robot wife, for the rest of my life.

Number 71 X 5 and 10.

Dark days

On those dark barren sands,
waves beating on breakers.
Cast out by a raging sea.
Seagulls' dip: plundering
natures fare.

Pebbles lacing along the shore,
like polished jewels.
Golden sandcastles melt away.
Distant memories,
of our happy yesterday.

A fog: laden horizon.
As a flickering lighthouse,
attempts to warn ships
along the bay.

The faint smell of fish and chips,
fragrances the air.
Reminding us of what fun we
had there.
As slowly, the rain
washes away.
All memories we shared on that bright
Summers' day.

The hopeful lover

Ever hopeful
Ever true
That is my love for you

The Kiss

I'm lost in your kiss
What love is this?
Enrobed in beauty; devoid of duty
What promise in that kiss?
So warm and beguiling
So strangely defiling
The magic of your, kiss!

Changing Places

Switched: divided at birth.
Our identities erased by thoughtless actions.
We were meant to be together, but the nurse
in her haste, slipped the name tag on the
wrong toe.
I saw my mother's sweet face, for but a
second.
Time to short for her to realise, that I
had been misplaced.
You were joined;
by a stranger who grew by
your side.
I no longer a double act but a solitary,
twinkling
light, lost feeling cold and half whole.
Destined to be alone.
We are not strangers,
but are linked by an invisible cord, that
our eyes cannot see.
I look for you daily, hoping that
each passing stranger may be you.
That's why I will not stop my quest.
Until our hearts, are in united rest.

Self Belief

I'm travelling down paths of discord.
Fearful, lonely and ignored.
They whose trust I thought I'd found.
Ignorant, lost, belligerent and blind.
Can they not see the blood that flows?
From the knives, that rip into my soul.
Mistrust the seeds they have sown.
Through countless lies spoken in
undertones.
Their faces tell too many lies of things
supposed, by me not them.
For I am but my only friend.
And I will not fear, for I feel freedoms
hand.
I know that this journey is at its end.
For I am but my only friend.

The Angel of Geary Lane

I walked down Geary Lane today,
And wished for a friend,
Someone to walk with me and love me just the
same
Amidst the dappled summer's light: that bright
sunny day.
I saw you sitting on a fence an Angel,
unaware.

Your wings, unfurled and brilliant white;
Shining in the sun, bringing love and hope
And true friendship to this one.

My Angel friend of Geary Lane;
Stayed with me all my life.
She told me I was never alone; and now she is
my wife.

The Letter

Crisp white: inked with words of love.
Folded neatly and enrobed in a papery carcase.
Entombed sentiments kept from view.
The scented envelope, holding its secrets
Until these words reach you.

Hands trembling, in anticipation
gently carry your paper form
to the awaiting post box, with it's open mouth.
I place you inside until you
are safely with my love.

Like a floating leaf, travelling through the air,
You travel through spaces,
people and places unseen.
Gathering memories and dreams,
before reaching your final destination.

Falling down through a hole in a door,
Slowly drifting down to meet a tiled floor.
Hands delicately lift your papery body lovingly,
held next to a beating heart.
Before being joyfully received with love.

In fields where we lay

Through battle lines,
a revelry of bullets
peppered the air.
Shouts, of anguish in the night.
Voices fearful, filled with fright.
Each of us knowing that
this could be our last.
As a bullet ripped from the
carcase of a gun.
Enters our bodies one by one.
Lights fade out, until
we are gone.
But still our memories
linger on.
For in a field
standing proud, poppies
tall and bold.
As blood red, reminders
of the lives that were shed.
Each lovingly remembering
as each, nods its head.

Unto my love

March bravely, my love
in to the arms, of the enemy.
Hold strong to happy memories,
of the love we share.

I wait for you in hopeful joy.
Longing for you to return,
and rest within my arms.

Days of endless wonder,
wishing for peace to return.
Knowing that you are far.
Wanting to be with you,
once more.
Far from the eyes: of war.

In Remembrance of Love

White lilies draped
on wooden boxes, of despair.
Eyes solemn cast: to the earth.
As we remember those we love.
Tears too many,
shroud fragile forms.
Shattered and empty.
As petals fall, like
peaceful snow.
We remember our love:
whole long ago.
Sweetly rest and heaven blest.
Safely home.

A Soldiers Love

We wait, in silence for the call.
I took your letter from my pocket,
and breathed each word.
Your fragrance stays with me,
I hold your words close to me.
All around me is chaos:
blood and the stench of war press
us closer to the enemy.
Just one more day, then we can
once again live.
As we go over the top, each life
to give.
For I shall see your face: no more.
My last breath, I give
to the end of war.

Anguish

With every drop of rain
I sign your name.
For a love like this,
Could never come.

With every drop of blood,
I feel the pain.
Thou I know not it's name.
Just the love that it has taken;
And the anguish that is to come.

As love lies bleeding.

The Silent Stealer

I miss you,
Tears fall, my heart lies broken on the kitchen floor
Why have you gone?
There are no words, but a cold silence
And the darkness: of the silent stealer.

I miss you,
It was only yesterday, that we enjoyed a fine sweet
wine
Why have you gone?
There are no words, just the sorrow of death
And the dark shadow: of the silent stealer.

I miss you, and my life is now incomplete.
Now, that the silent stealer has gone.

Perpetual Snow

He's numb from the waist down,
and doesn't care.

Why I love him?
I do not know

His love for me died long ago.

Like leaves covered,
in perpetual snow.

This love is breaking:
Row on row.

As ice forms at the
roots below.

This rosy smile:
a distant glow.

While this love lies
in perpetual snow.

Beneath my skin

He lives beneath my skin,
This stranger who's words;
I drink in like a fine wine
He lives beneath my skin
And entices and enthrals me; with his rhymes
Which make me feel sublime.
Oh, perfect stranger, how did I let you in?

You live beneath my skin
Your words drawing me and calling me from within
You live beneath my skin
Even though you still ignore me.

He lives within my skin,
This unrequited lover; unknown and silent
Now and forever
But I guess he always will.

Gagged!

Silently waiting,
looking hopeful
I dare not speak.

You cannot see,
can you?

For I have been silenced.

Though I speak,
you cannot hear
my voice.

The one within.

For she is gagged,
by him.

Now just a vessel
without a voice.

Silenced again,
though not by choice.

Storm winds

Turbulent winds: spiral delicate forms.
Sending debris, into dark skies.
Gathering in strength, building in force.
What once a quiet breeze holds prey
to fragile forms, tossing them askew.
Aggressively twisting in direction.
Distorting a pleasant vista, changing
what once had stood before.
Destruction and devastation, left
chaotically in it's wake.
As it rips through, the broken landscape.
Picking its path and flailing its victims,
scattering and shattering along its way.
Until silence is left, stormy skies dissipate.
Revealing a different vista, delicately laced
with yesterday's lost dreams.

Sweet Surrender

Sultry and sensual
Wistfully hopeful
Eagerly waiting
Each moment, wanting.
Tenderly, tempting.

Soulful, lamenting
Urgent and frenzied
Romantic and open
Remembering lovingly
Each moments, lovemaking
Naked and sincere
Dreamily, alluring
Entering, deeply
Recoiling, sweetly.

Secret Kisses

We steal kisses in places unseen.
Behind the village hall, and the old cow shed.
We deny ourselves, while passing on the village
green.
In case perchance that we are seen.

We text our words of love, all in code never to be
told
Hoping that they will never know
How far our love, I just don't know?

We steal kisses in places unseen
Though this is truly not my dream.

Valentine: Heart

Listen to my heart
It speaketh of love
For what of it?
Without it my heart,
Would surely break.
So I listen to my heart,
of sweet love notes doth take.
For my heart chimes;
I love you again and again
Oh! What a heavenly refrain
My heartbeats, I love you
again, just the same.
Thy sweet love, although I know not your name.

The Poet

I see the blank page afore me.
On what is the infinity curve: that is life.
And my pen inks these words, and breathes new life.
In to the stillness of the night, illuminating the
darkness
With a myriad, of words
To brighten the mind: and soothe the soul.
For the poet is the luminary a visionary fore told.

Silently scribing words, in the stillness of the night.
With shape forming artistry: to dazzle and adore.
To speak to the masses: a voice for us all.
The poet is a painter of the beautiful mind.
And from the bard, to the women I am.
I give thanks for the blessing I can.
To becoming this poet, I am.

You are: Life!

For the greatest pleasure, in life is just simply this:
LIFE!

To be electric with breath taking life.

There is know greater, than this your life!

So even in your bleakness, when all seems lost.

Never give up hope, for you are not lost.

For you are: LIFE!

Keep living, and being the dream.

There is no greater gift than your life.

Gratefully yours in love, and life.

Hoping that you keep strong.

Simply knowing that life is where you belong!

The Marathon

I catch my breathe at the starters gun,
running this race had just begun.
Steel hope and determination,
to win my cause: to feel the rush of the
applause.

Heart pounding, as I run
Hoping the pain, would refrain.
A willingness to carry on: and break
through the barrier.
Heart pounding, as I run
until my race, is won.

The jostle of bodies, running close by
some crimson and red, hearts pounding like
lead.
As we all race for our cause,
and not the applause.

Heart pounding, as I run
Until our race is won.
Then after the 26 miles have gone.
I know that finally my work is done.

Please Hear Me!

Back arched and twisted
Flesh bent double: contorted
He waits in silence
Dirty and unloved
Looking at each passer by.
Wondering why?
And longing to die
His hands reach out to touch your soul
As you walk by as nothings wrong
He simply wants to know your name
Feel loved and wanted just the same
But he is lost within the grime, of streets
so filthy and full of crime.
He needs love to my friend, for he was
once like you.
Until fate cleft him a deftly blow.
And left him homeless years ago.
So think for this man my friend,
as this could one day be you.

The Sound: to You.

You are the music,
the drum beat, the metronome.
Setting the tone.
Each note bringing, it home.
Your words and rhythm
swing me, and deep sing me.

You are the melody,
the harmony, sweetly enticing me.
Helping me, not to be alone.
Each lyric and line; penetrating my
bone.
Swing me: sweet music, sing to me.

You are the silence.
When, all the music has gone.
For you are, my song
and our music still goes strong.
As you swing me: deep sing me.

For this is the sound of our souls,
and the music will go on.
As you're sweet love sings me, and
brings me
to where our hearts are one.

The Heart of Words

Open your heart and let the words flow,
down into the waiting world below.
Like droplets of exquisite dew,
creating a rosy glow in all you do.

Let the words come - Poem one

I am an artisan, a rebel of wits
I am a traveller, an adventurer of the soul.
I am a clown, a bringer of joy.
I am a soul, waiting to be found.
I am, I am - YOU!

Let the words come - poem two

Like a rose, open me to the beauty of life
Like a drop of rain, falling into an ocean of
possibilities
Like a star shining in the night sky
I wait, I wait for you.

Let the words come - Poem three

I am the pen and you are my page
Let us write our beautiful music together
Let me ink my words of love upon your heart:
And keep them in your soul forever.

Let the words come - Poem four

Let the north winds blow,
But speak to me of love.
Let the dark night; engulf me in its blackness,
But speak to me of love

Please speak to me of love

Let the heat of summer's passions come,
But speak to me of love,
Of love, of love.
Oh! Come my love speak to me of love.

Please sweet love, speak to me of love.

The Twinkle of Love

The light of your love,
Twinkles like a beautiful star.
For you, my love
I love you, from a far.

Ebb and Flow

Today we live
Tonight we die
For this it twists
In blood and flow
Deep emotions
Letting go, of all the things
We used to know
Slipping by and letting go
Of love and life
We used to know.

The Shape of love

Your love is heart shaped
Bound with love
Tied with gossamer strands
To keep me close to you
Hearts beating together
But delicately held as one
Silently fusing and beating in time
Like a metronome
Joyfully beating
It's rhythm of love
So that our hearts
Will always be
One beat into your
Heart shaped
Love for me.

Broken

I cannot sleep.
For no more can I rest.
Half broken and crushed
by stress.
External forces conspire
hour by hour.
To drive us ever further
into some unending way.
Sleep deprived each passing
day.
Longing to be more
alive and living
No longer filled with
regret and misgivings.

Dying to meet you.

Wood on willow,
glistens against, breathless sinews.
As clouds of white,
role out across bland skies.

She waits, hopeful for a
new day.
Pain ravaging and twisting, the
creases of her newly ironed dress.

Intense surges wined through her
delicate form.
Against the heat of day.
She tries to breath, her last sweet
breathe.

White light: lights her way.
As she steps into a new
beginning.
Her brand new day.

Let me be free

Am I invisible?

Can they not see?

My need for sweet serenity

Has my sheer drop from grace
Landed me heavily upon my face.

Ground deep with in a quagmire
Devoid of peace that I desire.

They pull each strand, of energy
By clinging desperately to me.

I cannot breathe, know please let me go.
Too much you take, do you not know.

I am a person.

Let me be, unfettered
Independent and free!

Emergency!

From the stillness, chaos ensued.
Rushing: recklessly into a casualty room.
Raced, by ambulance.
Emblazoning: flashing lights.
Racing through the traffic; that cold
winter's night.
Paramedic pumping: to keep me alive.
Tubes and wires attached, to keep life on
my side.
I can hear my family saying, "Please do
not die".
Hoping internally, that this is a lie.
Emergency, please keep clear.
Hurried into resuscitation.
Hoping this was all but a dream.
As my heart: is fired back to life.
And my lungs,
gasp for air.
I am revived and glad to be alive.
Emergency resolved.
So grateful: to those saviours of my soul.
On that perilous cold,
winter's night.

Full Moon

The moon hangs in the sky.
Round and full.
Irradiating its power over the night,
in place of the heat of the sun.

Its craters visible and deep,
Eroded by time and filled
With the fragments: of space.
As it silently sits: oblique.
And like a timeless jewel
on the arm of space.

The light of the moon,
Illuminating the world below.
Lighting the darkness of the night.
Like a night watchman
Protecting earth's children.

Flow

From my pen, the stories ran.
Down pouring,
sweet flowing.
To catch each word,
my sincere plan.

Child of love

What is a child but borne of love?
A fragment of your heart, a voice that brings
new life: from sadness to joy.
You're blessing, of a girl or boy.
Who lights the corners of the night.
And fills your garden full of blooms.
Whose simple beauty you adore.
And to you their love is very pure.
Whose smiles chase darkened skies away.
You love them more each passing day.
And with you in their hearts, you'll always stay.

Come home to love

Carry me home, back
to the heart.
Wrapped in swathes of love
Bound with ribbons of hope
We wait for our love
To return
While they hope for release
And sweet surrender
Our hearts beat for loves
Sweet kiss
From the lips of those too tired to
Sleep
In our arms rest
Silent in silences
Slender peace.

The Weaver

Each thread taught
Wound and bound
Intertwined and woven.
Like webs of silken
Splendour, spun silently
In hands so tender.

Her breath rasps
Slow, as row on row
This vision of beauty
Starts to flow
The loom lags long
In dark seclusion
Her hands so red, and swollen
Bruised and broken
On arms that hang
As heavy as lead

Beautiful silks
Spun gold and flowing
Sold for more than
She is fed
While you adorned
In silken splendour
She lies now to
Weave no more.
Amongst the dead.

Love Words!

Love is you
Four little letters
Sang sweetly by
Four little birds
This song of my
hopeful love for you
Falls gently like
the snowy dove.
Each letter
is filled with love
Because my heart
is in your hand
There is no more
that I demand
Than simply just
to be your wife.
And love you
throughout your life.

I am One

I am one
A part of you, a part of me
The root, a seed of the old oak tree

I am one
A grain of salt, part of the sea
A whisper on the breeze

I am one
I
Am
One
You and me.

Wilfred

Death can hold you not.
For only time can tell
The tolling of true love
From the strength of the bell
Thou we walk in two worlds.
This you and I the next
We two bound in love now,
as we will in the next.

The Cracked Cup

Half full, flowing through
Small spaces
Golden shimmering remnants of you
This cup has lost it's meaning,
But not it's worth.

She takes the cup gentle
To her lips.
Amidst chipped rim and
tarnished glaze
Remembering those lost
Happy days

The cracks have appeared
over time.
To delicate China made
and used by heavy hands
with careless thought
This cup though chipped
Still hold's it's worth
For in those cracks lives
Love and care.

Weep no more

Drape softly along
Falling over your
Watery body
As it undulates
On rippled skin
Silent marks
Left as breathes
Of air lift
Your limbs delicately
And splay your appendages
Which break and fall
Battered by storm
Winds, you
Hold strong
Graceful and silent
Resting over calm
Waters.

Memories

This box is battered
and worn.

It's fragile and torn
But it's full of you.
Open the lid and you
Will see the joy it contains

The dreams we shared
Our memories
Know tied in ribbons
But not forgotten

Each word illuminating
All our past
For in this box
It holds our dreams that last

Our morning times
And dark nights
I love each memory
this imbues

As each piece here
Is filled with you
The love we shared
Is always new

This box I keep
close now, my lasting
memory of you.

Reflections of you

You pass me by
On the street
A complete stranger

But you look
Like someone I
Thought I knew
A vision of someone
Who could be you?

Eyes mockingly
Looking hopeful
Waiting to elicit
Your point of view
Shifting innocent
Reminders of you.

Chasing not knowing
If the picture
Is true
A moment's reflection
Of a girl I once knew.

Eternally Yours

I wrote a letter
hoping to find your heart.
Filling each line
with words of love
espescially just for you.

Each words inky
form reminds me
of you.
Not tidy as it,
slips from the page.

Thoughts dance across
the paper sowing
words of love.
And at the end,
I sign it with a kiss.
Eternally yours,
For that is what my
Love is?

Love

The sum of one
Holds the love of two
Hands held in a
Simple ring
Love is a blessing
An abstract of heart
A blueprint to follow
A pre-planned start.

Home

Follow my love
And you will see
The way to sweet
serenity.
To lift you up from
out of dark
To raise you high
 into the light.
No longer wondering
along your path.
Lost and alone,
but found at last.

A little bit about me the poet …

A little bit about me the poet...

I am Deborah M. Hodgetts, a poet, Author of Young Adult books, News Columnist, Freelance Writer, artist, photographer, Screenwriter and creative mind.

I live in a leafy village in the glorious countryside of Buckinghamshire, surrounded by beautiful nature, which always provides an abundance of creativity and inspiration.

I have been writing poetry and stories since the age of seven, after being greatly inspired by my wonderful mother, who used to skillfully write amazing poems and stories which she would regulary perform at competitions around my hometown of Staffordshire.

As a poet and creative writer I am eager to bring my gift of writing and creativity to the masses. I hope that the words contained within these pages, will inspire and uplift a new generation and make a huge difference in this World now, when it needs it the most.

To find out more about me and discover more healing words you can find me in the following places:
Twitter
Facebook
LinkedIn
Blog: The Beautiful Music of Words
I hope to see you again soon.

Deborah x

Lightning Source UK Ltd.
Milton Keynes UK
UKHW050355111122
411915UK00005B/142/J